MW01490497

Table of Contents

Dedication

In memory of my mom & dad,

Arthurene & Johnny Cook

My brother Peter "Eddie" Cook

and my grandparents

Acknowledgements

To the teachers and school staff who rescued me:

Mrs. Marian McKinney
Mrs. Ann Wood
Ms. Susan Pitcher

To those who assisted in the creation of this book:

Susan R. Coplan
Jeffrey Swan
Zaure Karabalina
Tone E. Fly

and to all the other Angels who
helped me along the way

Introduction by Robert Cook

My name is Robert Cook, and this is my story. It traces my life from my birth in rural Alabama to my life today at the opposite end of the United States: the Upper Peninsula of Michigan. Along the way, I stumble, fall and am raised up again. In some ways, this book cannot be my whole life story because our story is complete only when we pass from this life. I make no claim that my life is special or unique; I write these things mainly so that those who have experienced troubles like mine can know there is hope. Now, come with me on my "search for a purposeful life."

Chapter One
A Lost Child

    I was born by midwife to my momma on a
crisp March morning in Lowndes County,
Alabama, as the dew was leaving the grassy fields
and the sun was breaking the horizon. Although
some in my family say I was delivered the day
after, in our shack of a house, I was born on the
twenty-sixth. I was the baby of seven in our
family. I grew up chasing chickens around with
my brother Peter on the family farm. Momma,
dusted with flower, apron still on, and spoon in
hand would yell, "Don't you two be messin' with
those chickens, now."

    She didn't even have to see us kicking rocks
at the chickens to know we were up to no good.
Momma was a southern farm woman, so she

would be preparing chicken for dinner, starting by taking the chicken out back, then plucking the feathers out by the handful, real down-home cooking. She would come out on the porch, and Peter would be gone. He could run like the wind. I would run around the side of the house, which was raised up on bricks, and squeeze through a tiny hole under the porch to hide 'til momma wasn't so mad. When we got caught, and we always did, we would catch a whippin' for sure.

We were always up to something. Peter was a prankster and he constantly had me by his side. He was always coming up with ways to entertain and make people laugh. He would imitate daddy, strutting around with a hobble to his step, bracing himself on a stick, like daddy did with his cane. He looked just like daddy when he walked like him. Peter was the spitting image of daddy.

I don't remember exactly what I looked like. I've never seen a picture of me from when I was young. They say I look like a mix of both my momma and my daddy. I have momma's deep dark eyes and daddy's rounded chin with my big ole' ears sticking out. I used to get picked on for my big ears. I was small as a child, and with my ears sticking way out from my head the other kids would tease me. My brother Peter wouldn't stand for this. He would fight the other kids if they were mean to me. Life in Alabama didn't last long though.

When I was still young, momma died from kidney problems. I didn't understand death yet, I was only about five then. At the funeral my baby sister Jeanette and I tried to get into the casket with momma. We didn't know that this was going to be her final journey.

I was my momma's baby boy. I remember I would hide behind her legs and peer out around her apron at strangers when they would come by. I didn't understand that she was going and not coming back. I wish I could remember more of her features, like her face or her voice. I don't blame you; it's not your fault.

Daddy was working and couldn't stay at home with us kids. We started to move around to different family member's houses. We stayed at both our Grandma's homes for a short while, then my sister Lucille came down from Detroit saying that she wanted to take us. Daddy argued, " You can't take care of those kids!"—emphatic that she wouldn't be able to raise us right.

Hurt, Lucy responded just as emphatically: "Daddy, I'll take care of 'em. You don't need to worry; I'll look after 'em." So daddy reluctantly agreed to send us with Lucy to Detroit, and he would send her money every week.

My sister Lucy was older and married, with two kids of her own. She took us in, my brothers Bill, Peter, my baby sister Jeanette and I. Her two boys were great kids to be around. We always had a good time. We would dance around giggling as we watched the television dance-show, "The Scene" on summer nights. Fridays were our junk food days. We would go around the corner to the store and get candy and cookies. When I wasn't able to go to the store, my sister Lucy would always make sure that no one opened my cookies until I got there. I grew to love Charles and Pooh Bear as my own brothers. We don't know exactly what brought us to be as close as we were, with me being a few years older and all, but we did almost everything together. When I would catch a whippin' they would too.

They came to know me as their brother Robert. It took them into their teen years to remember I was Uncle Robert, not brother Robert. Pooh Bear explained it, "When you got older, it wasn't like you didn't mature as an adult, but you could still relate to us – you knew how to keep it adult with the adults and kid with the kids." Our sister treated us like one of her own, still there was a little more leniency toward us. Daddy was still our dad, though, so we all had to follow his wishes.

It got to a point, where Lucy sent a letter to daddy for more money, saying what she was getting wasn't enough. When my sister wrote that letter asking daddy for more help, he felt something was wrong and decided to come to Detroit.

"What made you come get us daddy?"

"I got tired of staying down south. After all, I had kids up in Michigan, so what was the use of me bein' in Alabama. I could have stayed and threw you kids away, but I wouldn't do that." He answered, "I am a man among men, not a mouse," as he often said. When he first came to see us, he saw how little we all were; we all looked like little racehorses! Our eyes looked like they were 'bout to pop outta our heads!

Daddy asked where the grocery store was, and Bill piped up, "Around the corner." So he took us there and got us two buggies of groceries.

"Just fill 'em up," he said. "Get whatever you want, whatever it is! And if that's not enough, get more!"

When Lucy came home she asked where all the groceries came from. "Daddy got 'em!" I almost yelled. I was so excited.

"Where is daddy?"

"Upstairs in the bed."

Lucy climbed the stairs, and turned into the bedroom. She was glad to see daddy too, "Daddy, you bought all these groceries?"

"Yes, I did. I thought you all was just drinking water."

He came down stairs and told us, "Y'all eat! Don't eat 'til yous get full; eat 'til yous get tired."

Daddy got settled in Detroit, and started work at the Ford factory. That was in his drinking days. If he got his check cashed and came down before he got drunk, he would leave some money, but if he started drinking that didn't happen. He came by one day, and went to the fridge for some water. "You all ain't got no food."

"Not really," was all Lucy could say. So he closed the door, drank the water, and left. He didn't leave any money for food or anything; he didn't help the situation.

Daddy decided to take us to his brother's house. It turned out to be one of many places we would stay for years to come. I don't blame you; it's not your fault.

Uncle had three kids of his own, all the family living in a three-bedroom house. I don't know how we all fit in there. There simply wasn't enough space for us all. When daddy finally got a house, I thought we'd all move in and have a home and a happy family again. I was wrong. Daddy drank a lot, and with the drinking came abuse.

Daddy started to have a lot of different ladies in his life. He was just lost without mom.

Living in the new house I got molested twice. The first time was by the sixteen-year-old son of one daddy's lady friends. I was only seven. I didn't cry or ask for help. Although I felt something was out of place, I did not understand what was going on. I was young, and I didn't have anyone there to protect me or tell me that what he did was wrong. The boy warned me not to say anything to my dad, which didn't matter. Daddy was drunk all the time and couldn't have helped me anyway. The second time it happened, it was the son of a different lady friend daddy brought home. There was no one to talk to about this, so after a while I just decided this must be the way things were supposed to be. Eventually daddy lost his house, and couldn't support us any more. My siblings and I later had to be split apart. My sister Jeanette was sent to live down south with dad's mother. I think dad sent her there to protect her. When he sent my sister away he sent away someone who was very close and dear to me. Peter was sent to live with another relative, and Bill left and went into the army.

I was constantly shuffled between the homes of different uncles and aunts. I had to move so much, because daddy was still getting drunk all the time, and wasn't taking care of my bills. He would constantly ask new relatives to take care of me for a little while. I don't blame you; it's not your fault.

One of my uncles I stayed with definitely believed what the Bible says about sparing the rod and spoiling the child. I would get beat not just for things I did wrong, but for whatever he felt like blaming on me. My cousins would fight with me and tell me that I was adopted. My one auntie was so mean. She was constantly telling horror stories in a creepy voice to make me scared of the basement where my bed was so I would fall asleep on the couch. Then she would have one of my cousins put cotton balls doused in lighter fluid between my toes and light them. It burned so, I couldn't walk right for weeks. I wouldn't feel safe to fall asleep anywhere in the house because of them. Sometimes they would tell me to go in my dad's pockets while he was passed out drunk, and take his money. I was sexually abused on multiple occasions. They would beat me and scratch me all up. One time my cousin even stuck my head in the oven in the basement and lit it, burning most of my hair and eyelashes off.

When I would stay at these homes, I was always afraid to ask for food, even a cookie or candy, because I would get punished, hit, or sent to my room. They would yell at me, "You just had something to eat!" But I would not be full, because there was not a lot to go around. The other kids' parents made sure that all their kids ate first. I was all alone. No one was there, no one to guide me, no one to guard me. So I would go to bed, praying that my daddy would come and get me. I kept wondering, "Why did my mom have to die, and why is daddy the way he is?"

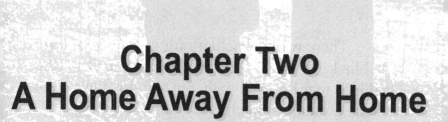

Chapter Two
A Home Away From Home

There was a sanctuary for me at the end of the block. It was the home of Abigail Hollis. She had kids that I played with, but she was the reason I stuck around so much. As soon as I got my chores done at Uncle's I would be back over at Abigail's playing. I was a smart-alecky kid and would curse Abigail's husband. He would tell me in his monotone voice, "Robert, if you're going to curse, you can't play in my yard."

Mockingly, I'd shout "I don't care!" back at him.

The next day I would apologize, "I'm sorry Mr. Hollis, I won't curse any more. Can I come and play now." I would sleep in Abigail's back yard so I would be close to the family. I'd sit on their porch for hours waiting for someone to come home. She treated me the way I thought my mother would. She would buy me candy, slippers, underwear, and anything else that I needed. She took care of me like she took care of her own children. That's when she adopted me as her Godson. When I was around twelve years old Abigail took me with her family to Cedar Point amusement park. We ran around there going on as many rides as we could. One ride, we came out of this long dark tunnel, and the track dropped a good forty to fifty feet into a huge lagoon and splashed every one of us, making us soaked to the bone, before the ride finished a few feet later. I had the time of my life. I acted as if I didn't have a care in the world.

Few knew what kind of life I had at Uncle's, but Abigail could sense something was wrong from how I acted. Abigail had a little cousin, Rianna. I met Rianna at Abigail's home. One day at Clayter Elementary School, Rianna saw me playing by myself in the sandbox and she came over to me and started talking with me. I was a stinky, nasty kid and rejected by the other kids. But Rianna saw something special in me and became a good friend. She also would come to my rescue when other kids would fight with me and pick on me, which was most of the time. The teachers would always put me in the corner and give me "time outs." They would say, "Something is wrong with this kid."

In junior high school, Rianna and I rode the bus together. Rianna would bring me to her house, take the time to help me to learn how to read and spell, and they would feed me and we would do talent shows. Speaking of talent shows, they held one at school and I was selected as the "King Robot" at Ricker Jr. High in 1977-78 (In case you don't know, the "robot" was a dance off Barry Jackson's "Dancing Machine.") I was doing well in school, and I became a "C" student. When it was time for high school, Rianna and I went to Saginaw Buena Vista, and that's when things started to get bad. We took a history class together, and the kids would tease me because I had trouble reading. Rianna would always come to my defense: "At least he's trying!" But we weren't together long. I had to leave. An uncle I lived with at that time didn't like a pair of baggy-leg M.C. Hammer" pants I bought, saying they looked like something a girl would wear. He hit me, and my dad took me out of my uncle's house and into his girlfriend's house. So I was off to a new school called Central Junior High in 1978. I was doing so badly; I was an E student. But somehow I got out and was on my way to Saginaw High School in 1979.

There, they did a Psycho-Educational Report. "Reason for referral: Robert recently moved to Saginaw from Buena Vista. Teacher reports indicate that school is very hard for him. Testing was requested to consider possible alternate educational programs for him. Test results: performance-borderline, verbal-borderline, full scale-bordeline. Slosson Intelligence Test: mentally handicapped, reading grade level: 3-9, spelling 2-7, key math 6-8. Summary and recommendations: Robert is a quiet, rather shy student to work with. When asked how he felt school was going, he said that it was going much better and that he didn't want to be placed in special education. Although Robert would qualify for placement in a special education program, his wishes should also be considered. Therefore, it is recommended that the EPPC consider that if Robert can find success in the regular program, he continue his present placement."

I was on my way back to Buena Vista in1979. By then, I didn't care any more; my head was so lost. People didn't know what was going on at home. Many suspected that not all was right, as I was a bad kid. I can remember that at my dad's girlfriend's house (where I was staying) there was a lot trouble due to drugs. I was sexually abused, too. I would cry and cry and say "Why me?" I just wanted to die. One time the police raided the place, and made us all lie on the floor. That's when I tried to use Abigail's address to get back into Buena Vista High School, but my uncle and aunt told the city I didn't live there. So it was back to Saginaw High. I never wanted to leave a place that became like home to me, but once again I was forced to leave.

Chapter Three
Finding Myself

In 1980 they put me in special ed. That's
when I really felt like an outcast, different from the
other so-called "normal" kids. But I loved singing
and dancing and they had a choir called the
Saginaw High Soul Choir. I auditioned for the
choir, which was directed by Mrs. Marian
McKinney—and I made it! Music had always been
my "out," my way to deal with the stress of my
family and surroundings. The soul choir was my
salvation, and at this time I met Troy Kempper. I
knew of Troy when he was twelve years old and I
was thirteen. I would see him at the Saginaw
Center. I admired him because he was taking
music and dance class with my cousin. Troy was a

major inspiration to me. He encouraged me to never give up, and he helped me to believe in myself. He helped me through that situation where my heart was broken and filled with so much pain. I did want to give up on life at that time. I know that God put Troy in my life for a reason. He was to show me that I can make it and that I will make it. He would say, "You have come this far, so let's not give up now. God has a plan for you to help someone. I know it gets hard sometimes, but hold on!"

Then I met Jeff Mason. He was a big guy who sang with us in the Soul Choir. I remember that he picked me up at first and tried to throw me over the steps. Troy laughed out loud and then we made our way to class. Then Jeff asked if we would like to go church with him, and we said yes. From then on we would always go to gospel worship together. We really became close when we were in school.

Mrs. McKinney was my angel. She would buy clothes for me and even pay my way on choir trips to places like New York and Chicago. Most important, she would listen when I needed someone to talk to and understand. I think that in a way, she saved my life at that time. I was supposed to graduate in 1981, but as I said earlier, they put me in special education class because of my learning disability. So I did not graduate until 1982. Through it all, Mrs. McKinney gave me encouragement, lifted my self-esteem, and genuinely cared about me. I remember one Sunday after church, I asked Jeff if I could spend the night, and I ended up living in his home for seven years. This was the first time I had a male friend that would not put his hands on me. I became very active in the church, and Jeff's family loved me unconditionally. Grandma and Granddaddy Mason, as I call Jeff's parents, had ten kids of their own, his sisters and brothers all accepted me as one of them, which made me excited and finally happy after such a long time, they took me under their roof and into all their hearts. Granddaddy Mason taught me everything from how to cut grass to helping build churches. He and Grandma Mason helped me turn myself around through the grace of God. I had been a mischievous child, but I became more loveable with their help and God's guiding hand. I really had a family. Now it is time for graduation, my sister Lucy from Detroit and my nephews were there and they gave me a beautiful graduation gift, a King James Bible, with my name stamped on the front cover, which I carry with me to this day. After graduation, I told Lucy I was considering going into the Army. She said, "Robert, if you want to go to school, I'll help you attended college." So I enrolled in small business administration at Delta College. I was doing extremely well, but I could not get transportation to school. I found a young lady I could commute with, but our schedules didn't match up. I became very depressed. I remember a time when I was really drunk, how Abigail probably saved my life. I was eighteen. I was so drunk that I was vomiting and even soiled myself. She took the time to clean me up and bathe me. Everyone else seemed so joyful, and I wondered, "What is wrong with me?" I did not want to be here on this earth. That was when I attempted suicide by taking pain pills. I started passing out, but I kept denying that I had taken the pills. I finally admitted it and they took me to the emergency room and I had my stomach pumped out. God was not read for me yet. The Mason family tried to help me as much as they could, and they constantly prayed for me. I got a job working for "Toys-R-Us." I flunked out of school. I could not handle the stress of school while feeling so down-in-the-dumps. That's when I became the choir director at Lighthouse Church, and it filled my spirit with hope.

Jeff's sister Alicia Preston became like my mom, because I would go to her house a lot. I loved her kids so much: Bethany, Malcolm and Marlow. Marlow and I were so darn close; we were like two little mice stuck together. I never liked white people as a child, but Marlow went to school with white people and he taught me to love all people despite their race, color, creed, or what have you. We are all one in the same. When I was in Buena Vista High School, the blacks would fight the whites-especially after the TV show "Roots" came out. Marlow helped me to understand that we all bleed the same color.

I would sleep on the floor just to stay by my brother Marlow. God sent a most beautiful person into my life in him. Marlow also taught me the importance of appreciating those who help you, even if they are not directly related to you. He taught me the meaning of a flower, a card, or just a note.

Then Marlow drowned. I tried to do the best I could to cope with his death, but I felt so alone. That's when I first tried alcohol and drugs. I needed someone to tell me, "You can do anything." Instead my grandmother said, "God works in mysterious ways, but he works in wonderful ways."

Little did I know just how true those words would be. The Mason family would actually become my real family. One day my dad knocked on Jeff's sister Lynn's door looking for me. Lynn was impressed with this dapper, handsome man — so much so that they began to date and eventually got married. Lynn, a single mother of six, and Johnnie Cooks, the man who had left behind his demons years ago, would become the perfect parents for all of us kids.

I was living in Saginaw with the Mason family and my dad while I went to beauty school.

It took a while to finish, but I did it! I flunked the written exam several times, but I passed the practical exams. My good friend, David, would always talk with me on the phone and would tell me, "Robert, let go and relax, because you have a beautiful gift and I know you can do it!" He was a special angel and I thank God for him. Finally, they let me get a reader, which was Rianna Warren. With her help, I passed the written test. I got my first job working for Sandra Bellefeuile at the 'Dare to Be You' Salon.

One day, I got a phone call telling me that my brother Peter went missing. Then they found him dead. He had been shot six times, and his fingers were cut off.

I wish my brother Peter was still here, but I know that he is still with me in spirit. When I think of Peter, I think of C.C. Winans' song "Don't Cry for Me". That's what Peter always told me when he was hurt or troubled.

Peter always told me that I had a great voice, and that I should be a singer. When he passed I decided I would sing at his funeral. The song was "How I Love You" by Rev. James Moore. I knew

God had sent that song to me. I remembered the words after hearing it only once. My aunt asked me, "Are you sure you're up to singing at Peter's funeral?"

"Yes, I know that's what he would have wanted me to do. He was my inspiration!" I stated as a matter of fact.

I was glad to leave the past behind me. It seemed like all the abuse I lived through was just a bad dream. Temporarily my life was at a quiet standstill. I was working at perfecting my skills as a stylist. I went to church regularly and directed the choir. Finding out who I was and enjoying my new family was my temporary lifestyle.

The Mason family home was a place where I learned all the good and sweet things about human nature. My new family healed a lot of my personal wounds, but life was still to show that I was dealing with huge emotional problems and confusions. I was still hiding in a closet regarding my sexuality, dating women who thought that my untypical behavior was just a result of a rough childhood. I was drinking regularly then. I wasn't able to let go and move on from my painful memories just yet.

I was in my mid-twenties when I thought of making a move to a bigger city with more possibilities. It took me some time to leave the nest, because I was still afraid of going out into the real world.

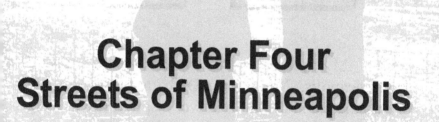

Chapter Four
Streets of Minneapolis

My journey led me westward toward Minneapolis, Minnesota. Barbara Smith, an old classmate and distant relative, inspired my moving there. Barbara had been living in the Minneapolis for a number of years. She told me one day over the phone, "Robert, you have a beautiful voice and I'd like you to meet some entertainment lawyers I know." Barbara also introduced me to Barry Reed, who had a thriving hair business in the Twin Cities. The idea was that I kept my hair career going while I worked on a music career, so that I could have an income. I talked with Barry on the phone and he invited me to come to Minneapolis. He even sent me the plane tickets. I don't think

Sandra B. and the folks at the salon expected me to make the "big move" to Minneapolis, but after working a twenty-four hour shift with Sandra for a telethon fundraiser, I packed up and left for the Twin Cities.

A three-hour flight landed me in Minneapolis International, and Barry and his friend Andy picked me up at the airport. We had never met before in person. Up came a man, slight-framed with an unkempt but sharply dressed look. With as much gusto and brazenness as he could muster puffing his chest out, he said, " Hi, I'm Barry!" With one hand slightly tilted up in gesture to stop right there, I said, "No. That's Barry over there." I was looking straight at him. Barry was leaning against the terminal wall looking all suave and debonair in his tight-pressed suit. "I know, because I've been talking to him for awhile."

I became an assistant to Barry in his beautiful and elegant salon. I stayed with Barry and Andy for about five months when I first got there, but when Andy's kids came to town I had to go and stay with Barbara.

The cosmetology laws were different in Minnesota, so I had to take another long test to get my cosmetology license in that state. And, oh yes, I flunked again—the first time. But Barry helped me, sending me to someone who could help me understand the Minnesota rules. Two weeks later, I took the test again at the University of Minnesota and passed it without a reader.

Now, I had my license and I was no longer Barry's assistant, but a stylist in my own right. Barry was impressed with the work I did, and started hooking me up with a good list of my own clients. But, there came a conflict between us. I would work all night doing hair and Barry would be done early for the day. Barry had assistants who helped him finish his work, and I didn't. I had the same number of customers as he did too, since I could do things that Barry couldn't with black folks' hair. This scheduling conflict threatened our relationship, so I told Andy that I would rather leave than lose my friendship with Barry.

I went to work for BBK's beauty salon, but I kept in contact with Barry. Barry had helped me and he loved me. I had a good job and a list of regular clients thanks to him.

Coming to Minneapolis gave me a good opportunity to discover my sexuality. At this time I was confused. I was still thinking that everything I experienced at home—molestation and rapes by male figures—was "normal." At this point I still wasn't educated about homosexuality.

Barry and Andy mentioned going to gay bars, and I followed the flow. Many men approached me. They would say that I looked "pretty", and "handsome". Looking at Barry and Ryan, a gay couple, I saw that they were happy. Happiness was what I was searching for. I enjoyed the company of older men, who were a "father" figure for me, a father that I always missed growing up.

That search took place at a bar called the "Gay 90s." The first man I met was Carl, 30 years older than I was. He helped and cared for me, but I could not love him the way he loved me. So I started drinking—a lot. While I was drunk, I would have sex with Carl, and then get up the next morning and start a fight. I would get so disgusted with him and myself. Then the same day I'd drink a whole bottle of liquor again, and go back into Carl's arms. I also did this because I would spend all my money on alcohol, and didn't have anything left over for rent. I had sex with him to have a place to stay; others I would sell myself to. I needed someone to love and to hold me, and, most of all, I needed my Dad. At this point the bottle became such a refuge for me, blocking out my shame and my painful memories.

I was always drinking at this point, just like my Dad used to. When I landed in Minneapolis I went wild. I was a raging drunk. I went to jail sixteen times while I lived there. I would be with "friends" who fought every chance they could. Not wanting to see the people I cared for get hurt, I would get involved. When the cops showed everybody split-up and ran. I would always get caught.

My last time in jail I was raped by two inmates. Their breath stunk of lust and their eyes were death. Bubba was in there for murder. Whenever asked about it the left side of his lip would curl into a deviously pleased smirk. He put that pillow on my head and whispered harshly, "Shut up. Don't you say nothin'!" The cell had only one little window the officers could see in through. My attackers knew exactly how not to get caught.

I got into drugs, heavily! I did more drugs than I am comfortable with. I knew it wasn't right; it just didn't feel right. I did it anyway. Carl couldn't handle it any more, and I don't blame him. So, I had to leave him.

The next man I met tried to kill me. Lying in bed, I asked him, "What are you all about?"

He went into the bathroom and returned with a stocking cap over his head, "This is what I'm all about!" He pulled out a knife and stabbed me as I lay there. I managed to knock him down, hit him with the lamp off the nightstand, and chase him out of the apartment.

I went back to Barbara's house and asked her, "What do I do? I have to go back to work and take care of my clients!" But, I couldn't work because of my injuries, so I left BBK's after I healed and I went to work at the salon "Studio 67".

I'd go back to the "90s" trying to meet another man, another father figure. Instead, I met a young man named Jamal. I thought that I had met my real love. Truth be told, he had problems of his own. He was, like me, an addict. We would spend our evenings drinking and doing coke 'till early morning and fighting the whole way through. Jamal constantly lied to me, but I would find out the truth, which made me angry. I would do everything for him, not caring about myself. He was not the "dad" figure I had been seeking, being quite a bit younger than I was.

One night, while trying to get inside my apartment after being locked out by Jamal, I smashed a glass door, and cut my wrist. I was drunk and all coked-out that night. I cut a main artery and three nerves. When the ambulance came down, the paramedics said that I was just lying in a puddle of blood that was gushing out of my wrist. There was still a chunk of glass stuck in the gaping wound. The doctors said that it might have saved me, blocking from too much blood loss. They also said that I would be paralyzed. I think mom was watching over me that night.

Everyone was amazed that I regained the use of that hand, although I suffer when the weather gets damp. I block out the pain; I'm good at that.

I couldn't work because of my injury and soon started to lose everything. Jamal was long gone by then. I fell months behind on rent, and I had to go to court. I was soon homeless and lost my job. That's when God sent me Tomas.

Tomas was an angel of God that gave me a place to stay in Minneapolis so I wouldn't be homeless. He was interested in me at first, but he did not know of my inner pain. When he learned of it, the idea of a relationship stopped right there. Also, I told him I just wanted a brother. He was a true friend. He let me stay in his apartment and I found work at a nearby salon called "Sumayah's Palace of Beauty." That's when I started to be happy again, there was beauty within the palace! Later Tomas found himself a friend, moved out and left me his apartment. We remained good friends. That same year, his brother came by my place to let me know that Tomas died of AIDS.

It seemed like my only friend in Minneapolis was gone when Tomas died. The floodgates were opened on the alcohol. I started drinking heavily and steadily, and at this point I met my neighbor Gary across the hall. I thought at first that he would replace Tomas, but Gary introduced me to the drug crack cocaine instead. That first hit of crack made me see a bright shining light in my eyes. What I saw made me realize something wasn't right. I wasn't right. I had drifted away from Him, and He had shown me this through that light. Instinctively I called the first person I could think of for help, my Aunt Peg back home. She stayed on the phone with me for hours and prayed with me. Her words of wisdom and encouragement brought me out of that place of worry and brought me into peace. It wouldn't last, though. Eventually I would be back to my typical ways of boozin' and abusin'.

There were people in the salon that could see changes in me; they knew something was wrong. A customer named Dr. Ibura-I called her "Doctor Mom"—told me right out, "Robert, you're letting the devil take control of your life." I had to tell her the truth as to what I was doing. I wasn't fooling anyone, except myself.

Around this time I met Tiffany. I always wanted a child, and God sent me a beautiful daughter in Tiffany. I met her at a modeling competition when we were both chosen by a modeling agency in Minneapolis. We had some acting classes together and saw more and more of each other. She modeled for me while I worked Sumayah. We went on a modeling competition trip to New York, with a group, and had so much fun together. I like to give people nicknames, and I gave everyone on the trip a nickname, except Tiffany. I had something special in mind for her. The name was "Angel." She truly is my angel to this day.

Tiffany would come and stay with me at my house, but I was concerned what her parents would think. She was a major blessing in my life. She helped me gain the acceptance to know that I needed help regaining control of my life. She was only sixteen when we met, and although I looked at her as my daughter I was afraid her parents would not understand. I eventually met her mother, who told me that Tiffany was adopted. She also told me I even looked like Tiffany's real father! She gave her blessing to our friendship, and I talk to her to this day, and call her Ma'. Tiffany grew up in front of my eyes, and I love her, she is my Angel.

I had to ask for help because I was tired of feeling so alone and ashamed. I chose to go into a treatment center called Affirmation Place. There was a young lady I met in the salon; a judge named Pam Alexander. I told her I didn't have any insurance, but I wanted to go to treatment. She said, "I can get you a Rule 25. A Rule 25 allows you to get treatment, even without insurance, because it is funded by the government."

I went to Affirmation Place and was doing well, but I was still living in the downtown area of Minneapolis with people who said they were my friends. They were not my friends. They knew the weaker side of me, and led me back into my old habits. I knew I was an alcoholic, but they argued, "Oh, no. You're just having a good time, just being yourself. You're fine." Deep down inside I knew there was something really hurting me, but I couldn't find it 'cause there were so many chemicals in my body. My mind had become lost and I did not care any more.

While at Affirmation Place I learned many valuable tools. One of those tools is the personal affirmation. A sample list and general guidelines are in appendix A.

There was so much pain for me on those streets. I'll never forget being locked in a crack house—for months at a time! I was held hostage twice. They would bolt the doors from the outside when they would leave. After so long they slipped up and didn't lock the door all the way. I managed to sneak out.

I went back to the Gay 90s, still looking for that father figure. One night while there, I met a man who I call my true angel—Don. He was from Michigan, like me, but a place in Michigan I had never heard of—the Upper Peninsula. We exchanged phone numbers, but I never really expected to hear from him again. But he did call back. Don was looking for someone too. He was not searching for a father figure, but a friend to settle down with. I wasn't sure I was ready. Don kept calling and visiting, and our relationship really started when Tomas moved out and left me the apartment. He eventually took his furniture, leaving me with a bed and TV and not much else. Don and I decided we would furnish the apartment, and that's when it began to feel like we had something deeper than just a casual relationship.

I remember my first visit to the U.P. It seemed so far from everywhere! That was over Thanksgiving. Don wanted to make sure that I would not be spending the holiday alone in Minneapolis, and he wanted me to meet his family, which was soon to become my family. Don had also picked out a car for me, a Buick LeSabre, and we would drive it back to Minneapolis, then he would fly back to Escanaba.

We had Thanksgiving at Don's brother Greg's house, and because Greg's wife Debbie had her own beauty salon in her basement, it wasn't long before we were down there, and I was restyling Don's sister Jean's hair! I was nervous at first about meeting my new family, but I shouldn't have been—we hit it off right away. I would return that Christmas, and for many more family gatherings afterward.

I first met "Mom Josie", Don's mom, on the telephone. I would call her and act crazy like I do sometimes on the phone, and call her "ma". She told me later that she almost hung up on me at first, until Don told her who I was. I remember the first time I saw her. I walked into the house just before that first Thanksgiving in Escanaba. She was sitting on the couch, reading and looking so tiny! Since then, she has had some small strokes and can't get around or talk like she once could. I feel like it's my special purpose to make her life beautiful, so I take her on walks and cook and clean for her. I also tease her a lot; she says I drive her crazy! But when I go for a few days, she always says, "I missed you, Robert" when I return. Don says she really enjoys the teasing, because his dad was a big tease and I remind her of him, in that way. We had a nice drive back to Minneapolis, stopping in Rhinelander, Wisconsin for the night.

Don was too far away to keep me from getting in with so-called friends like Gary, and once I had a car, I found that I had many of them.

Most of them were looking for rides here and there, like to the bars downtown. It was inevitable that I would start drinking again. One night, I hit something—I don't remember what—and I damaged the front end of the LeSabre so that it couldn't be driven any longer. Don eventually came to Minneapolis, got the car and got it fixed up so it could be sold to pay off the loan. I quit working and was spending a lot time hitting up my friends for money to buy drugs for "my brother" Gary.

One of the bright spots during this time was Casey. I met Casey at a modeling competition. He moved in with me, and I had found a "little brother." I didn't want Casey to follow in my footsteps doing all the destructive things I was doing, like drugs and drinking, so I opened up to him about my addictions. Casey and I decided that we would have to get out of Minneapolis, as far as possible from the drug scene I was into. That's when we started looking for a house to rent.

At first, we looked in the suburbs, but the prices were too high. That's when Don came up with the idea of buying a house. He had it all figured out. Eventually we found a beautiful split-level home in Plymouth, MN. It was about twenty miles away from Minneapolis. We moved into the house over New Year's and I had a special "nationality" dinner party. We had such a peaceful and happy time once we moved in. Don and I took so much pride furnishing the house in beautiful off white colored furniture!

While at the house I got to drinkin' again and getting high off weed, and that made me want an even bigger high. Plymouth was not far enough from Minneapolis. I found Gary again, living in a nearby suburb. I went back to my old behavior, drinking and doing drugs.

The drinking and drugging drove a wedge between Casey and me and he moved out—leaving me all alone in that big house. I wished Don could move there, and he even interviewed for a job at a radio station in Minneapolis, but his family—especially his mom, who had recently had a stroke, needed him in Escanaba.

I needed to work, and I found a job at an Amoco station not far from my house. At first, they didn't want to hire me, but a big guy named

Steve said, "Give this guy a chance." So I went to work—walking both ways in all kinds of weather because I had no license due to a DWI.

I worked at the station with a young man named George Dean. We invited George and his friends to Don's 50th birthday party, which we had at the house. George became a great friend and a brother to me. He would come over and have talks, and he looked up to me. I saw he was headed down some of the same paths I had gone down, and I tried to talk to him. I did not want him to make the same mistakes I had. I found out that George had a drunk driving accident where someone almost died. He felt lost and angry with himself. Through our conversations and prayer that young man made it through those tough times. We still talk today.

Chapter Five
Mr. Happy is Born

What can I say about Mr. Happy? He is a character I invented while working the overnight shift at the Amoco station in Plymouth, Minnesota. I used to listen to KDWB radio, and to the overnight DJ, J.J. Kincaide. I always got a kick out of the characters that would call in to his show; they seemed to have a lot of fun, and so did J. J. So one night I decided to call him and try to win tickets to a KDWB event known as the "Star Party." J. J. liked my crazy, positive character, and he said, "You can call every night. We'll call you Mr. Happiness." Well, I shortened the name to "Mr. Happy", and it stuck.

Mr. Happy is best known for his crazy laugh and trademark phrase "...and you know this Love!" He talks about everything. He talks to those who need advice, are lost, or just need to share. Mostly it is fun stuff — talk about the new wheels on my car, or the troubles Mr. Happy got into at a Minneapolis bar when he and his friend "Little Happy" had a little too much to drink. Sometimes, it's serious stuff-like when I talked about my rehab at Pride Institute and my struggles with drugs and alcohol. Some other topics included getting adjusted to life in Escanaba, Michigan, going back to college as an adult, my relationships with people and family. Usually, JJ and I decide on a topic for the day-and let it fly to wherever it lands! It was natural that I should develop a character like Mr. Happy. I love to entertain, and I'm not afraid to "get personal" on the air. People really appreciate someone who's real.

Through the creation of Mr. Happy, my life was saved. He talks people through tough times and keeps focus on the positive. He is exactly what I needed. Through creating Mr. Happy I have been able to meet so many good people. They would come to the Amoco station where I worked just to meet Mr. Happy. It was as if God was sending angels to guard me.

I must have made a big impact on the KDWB overnight show, because it wasn't long before I would call at other times of the day and get put on the air! I even did bits on the *Dave Ryan in the Morning* show and the afternoon show hosted by Tone E. Fly. Tone E. also had a show for a time in Pittsburgh, Pennsylvania and in Austin, Texas for a time and I did regular bits there as well. We're real brothers, Tone E. and me. He's back in Minneapolis working at 96.3 NOW. Often I will call him to talk things over or get advice off the air, and he's always ready to listen.

When I first met Tone E., I thought he was the most arrogant, stuck-up person that you could imagine! But I thank God for sending him into my life, because he has become a true friend. We have the most beautiful time together. He knows all about my personal life, the pain I have been through. There was one time that I wanted to give up on Mr. Happy, but he said to me, "You are always talking about God and spirituality and reading your Bible; why give up?" I needed that guidance, because it showed me how much I am loved.

There was a period of time where I wanted to give up on Mr. Happy. Satan kept knocking me down. But, I realized that God had sent his son Jesus to free us from the shackles that would hold us back. With the wise words of my good friend Tone E. Fly and the uplifting hands of Our Father, I kept on.

One of the regular customers at the Amoco station where I worked was an awe- inspiring woman by the name of Kris. She was an angel, one in a billion. She walked into a room with such confidence. Kris controlled any situation she put herself into, by force if necessary. Even in the darkest hours, she showed me the light of her beautiful chestnut eyes. Her coming into my life started a change in me, but the change wouldn't take place overnight. Kris saw all the things I was going through and took charge, as a mother would. Kris was a woman with so much honor, and she knew through her wisdom she would be respected.

Having created Mr. Happy truly saved me at this point. The stories I would call in to KDWB with began to change from the wild nights remembered through a haze and a headache, through the battles I fought with temptation, to the memorable moments of each and every day and how joyous they all can be.

Don and I went through all the "hoops" and got my license reinstated, and we went car shopping. We eventually settled on a Honda DelSol that we bought in St. Paul. I think it was Don's choice because it's a convertible, and he loves convertibles. After I got a car, it was easier for me to get to the drugs. I would get that first 'rush' from drinking, and I'd want to keep the "buzz" going after the stores closed. So I'd head for the crack houses in the city, and I would meet men who would want to have sex with me. I'll never forget one crack house, where the people seemed nice. Before I realized it, it was 2 a.m. and they had taken my car. I was afraid to call Don because I had told him I wasn't doing that stuff anymore. Thank God that one man there felt sorry for me. He got me in touch with a friend, who took me to her home and said, "Don't worry. We'll get your car back." She also said, "You need to go to meetings, or it's not going to get better." I said, "Okay." But I didn't go; I was still in denial.

When I got another DWI, Kris said, "Robert, you're going into a treatment center." I broke down and cried. Kris was like the mom I had lost so many years ago. She said, "Get some rest, and we'll take you there tomorrow."

But the addict was still in control. That night I was drunk and got into my car to go for a ride. The police caught me and took me to jail. I called Kris and she already knew. She felt something bad was going to happen and had come back to my house earlier to get my car keys. When I wasn't there she figured out what had happened. The judge had decided to put me in jail for 500 days, but Kris convinced the court that I needed treatment instead. "I know him and talk with him; he's like my little brother," she told the judge. The judge listened and dropped the 500 days, instead sending me to treatment at Pride Institute, where I remained for 31 days. Pride Institute was chosen because it is a gay-oriented treatment center and would help me deal with the sexual issues that were part of my drinking and substance abuse problems. Kris came to visit me every Sunday and I locked away many of my old friends. "That's fine," she would say. "You don't need them anyway."

As we talked in our reflection group at the treatment center, I decided to move to Escanaba to live with Don and go to college. I would be with my "other family" for love and support.

Chapter Six
Escanaba

Living in Escanaba was a big change from my life in the big city. I started taking a few classes at Bay de Noc Community College, and met many positive people. It was a good change for me.

At Bay college I met Zaure, a young lady from Kazakhstan, who later became my friend. I first met her while waiting outside the door to my English class, having no idea that she was the tutor I was supposed to meet later that day. Her eyes smiled at me. She was tutoring her friend from her country who was in my class, and she said to me, "Be nice to my friend, and help her if you can because her English is not that good." Later on, all of us—Zaure, her friend, and myself—used to have study groups at the library and talk and spend time together. Sometimes we didn't even get any homework done! Zaure is from another country, so she was often confused about our culture and I helped her with that. I told her that I wanted her to preserve her own culture, and stay happy as she was, but also pay attention to everything going on around her. We laugh to this day as she tells me that I helped her so much, but sometimes I would confuse her even more with things I said!

Zaure even got me involved in Model UN. The Model UN group took a trip to South Dakota, which was a lot of fun and allowed me to make new friends. We lobbied in favor of Zaure's home country, Kazakhstan. Since I was majoring in social work, I was assigned to the social council board. I was on that board alone, lobbying against two other students. I won that part for our school. I did well in the Model UN and at Bay College.

I must say that the UP was nothing like any place that I lived in before. It has a country style living, not unlike in that movie *Fargo*, where the city is surrounded by woods, has beautiful nature and country air. People call it "God's Country."

During the summer of two thousand one, I took a Caribbean cruise and spent a lot of time networking with people from all over the world. Mr. Happy has extended his presence well beyond Minneapolis, Austin and Pittsburgh, where he has appeared on the radio. I made sure they got Mr. happy business cards, with his Web address. It was great fun checking out my guest book as it filled with messages from just about everywhere. I still keep in contact with many of my new friends.

Through YouTube Mr. Happy has increased his presence worldwide. I now have fans all over the world! There are fans in Ireland, Spain, Tokyo, and more join every day from anywhere and everywhere in between

I guess the small-town atmosphere bored me. My one outlet was a Casino about fifteen miles west of town. I figured, "I like it out here, so why not apply for a job?" I was hired just before my second year of school would have started, so I decided to delay school and work full time as a "Keno runner." Keno runners go through the

Casino selling Keno tickets. It was a perfect job for me, as I got to meet a lot of interesting people and practice my selling skills. I also started going to AA meetings so I wouldn't go back to my self-destructive ways. I had to realize that I am an addict and any little setback can easily turn you back to that life.

Then a lady—a casino employee—said I sexually harassed her while I was off duty. She made a complaint, and the next thing I knew I was terminated. It was her word against that of a gay black man. When I filed for unemployment, the casino objected and it was denied. So I hired an attorney and he got a hearing, but the judge decided in favor of the casino. He said I could appeal his decision to the local circuit court, but my chances weren't too good, so I dropped it. If you have a discrimination complaint, you must bring it to their courts and their judges decide it. At one point when a customer referred to me by the "n" word, casino security just laughed it off. In any other business, the customer would have been ejected.

While I worked at the Casino, we had a lot of tension among the employees. They called a special meeting, and I wrote a poem to help express my feelings. It's titled "Why?"

Why do you come to work having a bad day, and make everyone else have a bad day also? Why do we smile at each other's faces, then laugh behind each other's backs? Why do we intimidate one another? Why do we claim to be team members, then talk about each other to our customers? Why do we try to make a person feel inferior? Why do we bring a joyful person down? Why do we bring our personal pain into our place of employment? Why do you say we are team members, then fail to support each other? Why do you say, 'I am better than you?' Please tell me, why? I hurt, I cry, I bleed and I feel pain just like anyone else, but I choose not to bring that to my co-workers or my customers; they are the ones that bring me joy. You don't need to like me, but I demand to be treated with the same respect I show to you. Why do you try to make me feel like I am always to blame? Can't you see inside yourself that you may have done something wrong? Why do I always have to apologize? Why can't people compliment each other when they are doing a good job? Why do we need to make others feel small? Why has the laughter and joy turned to negativity, pain, frustration and jealousy? Can you please tell me, why? We are a team and should be uplifting one another, not bringing down each other! Why do we not ask, 'I wonder what cup of coffee he or she had this morning? Can I have a taste or a bite of your joy?' Why do we have to take a knife and stab one another so deeply into his or her back? If the shoe fits, do not be afraid to wear it! We can and will get greater if we answer these questions…Why?"

After I was terminated from the casino, I moved to Menominee, which is a town about sixty miles west of Escanaba. Menominee is an almost all blue-collar workers' town. I'll never forget how many names I was called—names like nigger. I am honored that I had the education of Bay College to teach me the definition of those words, and the fact that God was in my life, so I could pray for their salvation. Trust me, it hurt to hear those things, like a threat to tie me to a truck and drag me down the road. I would just keep on walking, and smiling and praying the twenty-third Psalm: "The Lord is my shepherd, I shall not want."

But I also met some very lovely people there. Like Trish. I met this young beautiful lady while I was doing hair at the Regis Styling Salon in Marinette, Wisconsin (across the river from Menominee). She walked in and I knew just by her eyes that she had a powerful spirit. Trish ran a place for battered women called The Rainbow House. I told her I would like to volunteer my services to help get these women go back out into the world and, in some cases, to find work. I would do it by making them feel beautiful and confident. It is so wonderful when you can help someone else. My stay in Menominee was not for too long. I lived there for only about a year before I moved back to Escanaba.

Before I left, though, my brother decided to throw me a party for my fortieth birthday. It was such a blessing. We held it in Peshtigo, a town midway between where the majority of my friends lived. I had all my family there and I gave thanks for my "Angel of Light" party. I also invited the people who had called me names and threatened me. They all showed up. They are now some of my closest friends. I moved back to Escanaba to live with Don.

I got to drinking again. My last incident that brought me into recovery happened shortly after my Granddaddy passed. After his funeral I came back to the U.P. and became very depressed. I bought some beer and took it home and drank it. I don't know why I decided to leave the house after I had been drinking. The rain was pouring down in buckets. It would have been hard for even a sober person to drive. I hit a parked car, demolishing it, and the front grill of the car I was driving ended up inches from my lap. I thank God that no one was hurt by what had happened. I realized that I would have to go into treatment immediately to deal with my alcohol and substance abuse. I learned to deal with stressful situations without the "help" of alcohol or drugs in treatment. I realize that my recovery will never be complete, that I must resist alcohol and drugs one day at a time with the help of God and good, sober friends.

I know it's going to take time for these wounds to heal, 'cause I've been wounded so much. Sometimes I want to give up, but I cannot. I will not give up. Mr. Happy spreads love all over the world. There are so many people who have been wounded and have been through much worse than I have. Many are not here to talk about it and touch someone else's life. The reality is that this world is full of heartache and hardships, and we must all have the strength journey through it with our heads up.

I thank my step-mom for teaching me that can not is not true. It gave me the ability to accomplish anything I approach in my life. I was in Saginaw helping my mom after my daddy had passed when she had me run her store Elite Diva. I ran that store for the better part of three years. It was by God's grace and mercy how he brought me back. Being able to get to know all my customers and help them feel better energized me and made me feel anew. I was on my way back to Escanaba when my Ma' said to me, "You know Rob, I have this store and you are such a people person. I want you to run it." I never realized that she was watching me so closely. I felt so beautiful. It brought me into a spiritual light. It was like when I was at Lighthouse church. Through her being so positive and filled with the Holy Spirit and the Love of Jesus, she believed in me. I thank her for believing in me. We encourage each other through Father's Day every year it passes and my daddy's not here. She taught me many skills needed in business and in life. I thank God for bringing such a wonderful mother into my life.

Chapter Seven
The Blind Man

There was a blind man walking in a bright light, looking to find a wonderful place, looking for forgiveness for his soul. That light became a light for all to see. Knowing that he could have stayed in the dark, knowing the human limitations that cannot fully comprehend God's love in that light! Praying to God to make him wise and strong and with all his faith that he would come out of that blindness one day.   You see a man who respects intelligent men and his love for the world. He seeks to become better and to express beauty by his wisdom: knowing beautiful treasures are in that light; knowing that no one knows but God!

Today, I found the truth about what is in that light for me to see. I just need to put my sense of humor into effect and lower the filter between brain and mouth, called consciousness.
Sometimes, I feel tired of it all. It would be great if I could have a healthy balance and be more comfortable with myself.

I've been hiding in that light, blind to my own soul, hiding with that disease called HIV for how many years? Eighteen years! Lord willing, I want to help others: to show them how you can stay free and alive through many years of this disease.

I was first diagnosed with HIV in Minneapolis in 1994 during a three-day hospital stay. I had kidney stones, which I thought were caused by cocaine use. That's when I was told that my T-cell count was greater than 1,000, but medications for HIV were not recommended at that time. For many years, I had no special care or medications, keeping my trust in God.

I first started feeling ill while working in Marinette, Wisconsin in 2003. I went to a specialist for a consultation. At that point, my T-cell count was 1,629 and my CD-4 count was 350. If my CD-4 had dropped to 250, I would have had "full blown" AIDS. That was in May 2003. A month later, the doctor put me on the "miracle drugs" Combivir and Sustiva. Since then, I have had a checkup about every six months, until by 2011, the HIV became undetectable. In fact, my doctor wrote on July 11, 2010: "Your viral load was undetectable...and your CD count is 905. And on May 5, 2011: once again, your viral load was undetectable. And no virus in your blood. This is extremely good news."

Do I know who gave this disease to me? No, I do not. I just know that I was drunk and drugged out on crack cocaine, speed and acid. I just wanted to feel loved, and someone gave it to me. This disease hurt me extremely badly, and I wanted to hurt others. I did not care about myself any more; I did not want to live. I was ashamed. I felt nasty, like a dirty, filthy rag. But I came to understand more about HIV, and I told my doctor, "I will be one of your advocates." I know that God put me on this earth to help all, especially the young, to be careful what they put into their bodies. It can take away your mind and your ability to make the right decisions; just say no!

HIV is just a virus, like a cold. Your immune system is already weakened, and drinking and drug use will make it worse. I did a lot of research on this. I had to stop the drinking and drug use because I wanted to live. And so by knowing all these things, I can help others. My immune system is strengthened and my T-cell count is near normal. I need to be an advocate to help others. We all have to go into the world to give our testimony. There are so many choices in life that are destructive.

I am so happy that I am not blinded by the light any more, and that I can shine my light on a good path for others. I am also thankful God has sent good doctors and nurses to me. HIV is really a blessing, and like the Apostle Paul, I will glory in my infirmity and use it as a way to help others.

Reflections of Love
A Song by Robert Cook

You were not a mistake, for all your days are
written in my heart
I have always been your love and will always be a
reflection of your heart
We can find no more appropriate words to use
In introducing this volume of reflections of love
Reflections of love!

Today is absolute certainty
My creator has entered into my heart
Commenced me to accomplish all the love
That you could possibly imagine
Now in my heart you are my treasured possession
I pray, I pray, I pray for peace
To stay in my heart

I love you for your grace
As the pain I carried in my heart!
I keep you in my heart
Close, close to my heart

And as each day comes, I will always be filled
with your love
I am a brand new life!
My, my question? Will you be my child!
Waiting for you, I meet your needs
'Cause I am the reflections
Reflections of your love!

Pooh Bear Says...

You can't let anyone else's negativity be a
reflection on how you go; you've got to take
their negative energy and pray about it and do
better from that point on. You can't depend
on nobody but yourself. You block your
blessings by harboring that anger from the
past. You gotta press on the best way you
can. You've got to use your mind without
any kind of controlled substance—get this
energy. You might think you're having fun,
but when the walls come crashing down your
"friends" won't be there—you're all alone.
The easiest thing would be to end it, but
someone comes along and saves your life.
After I lost everything, I was going to jump
off the Belle Isle Bridge, but someone came
along for me—even if he didn't know it. He
didn't really talk me out of it—just asked,
"What are you going to do?" I decided I
didn't want to be in the past no more,
mentally or physically. I wasn't going to take

myself out for someone who really never
cared for me in the first place.

Epilogue
Head Held High

In my life I feel empty. I feel alone, but I know I'm not alone because I know what Jesus said, that he wants me to face reality. We have to realize that we are human, and I remember what my Father said; that he would take me through tests, trial, and tribulations. But only the strong shall survive. I also remember what he said to Paul, "Keep your mind on me and I will keep you in perfect peace." I am honored to keep my mind on Him, and to keep growing stronger in His grace and mercy every day.

He wants me to face the reality of life, and this story of emptiness is one I have to tell. I am constantly in pain, but I am not desensitizing myself with alcohol or any other drugs. I realize that I am just a "dirty, filthy rag". All the tragedies that have happened in my life I was blocking out for years. Hiding behind the bottle, a crack pipe, and whatever else I could find that would take my mind off reality. It's hard to block it, I mean He wants me to face the pain and the emptiness. He wants me to face the day with my head held high. Through the trials and tribulations I have been through, I now can. I have quite a few good, beautiful friends in my life. I call them my angels, and they are angels from God.

I will never forget the time I was out to dinner in Escanaba, and a little girl at the restaurant cried out, "Mommy, mommy, look—a Black man!" Did I feel offended? No! I went up to that little child and introduced myself to her. I said, "Yes, I am Black, but my name is Robert."

She responded, "The only thing I ever saw that was black was a black cat I had, and the eyes popped out!" I laughed.

Another time, when I was taking mother Curran on her daily walk, a man yelled, "Look at that nigger!"

Mother Curran showed me through her confidence that she was not racist and she blocked it out of her mind. I know that she was praying, "Forgive them Lord, for they know not what they do." And that's what I was doing too. It gave me the confidence to walk with my head held high. "Nigger" means that you are stupid. That word is not welcome in my vocabulary. No one person should be made to feel stupid or inferior to another. We are all blessed with a special talent or gift.

Jesus said, "If you want to see me, see me through other people." It's with that I remind y'all about that little girl. She saw me with the love of God in her innocent eyes and a little amazement too.

My girl Raquel, or mama sister, is a true righteous woman of God. She helped me through many of my trials, including the deaths of those close to me. I'll never forget how she helped me when I was locking myself away in my home.

Raquel is a sweet woman. I call her each and every day. She understands me. There are not many people who can finish one of my sentences, but she can. I used to ask her, "Why are you so friendly to me, so nice?" I had been wounded so. She would tell me, "Rob if I tell you I'm a friend, I'm a friend!" She got me out more and kept me from locking myself in a box. I am truly thankful for her and all of the good people in my life for helping me deal with my emptiness.

I give all thanks to God for bringing Mr. Happy into my life, to be like His son Jesus—to love all mankind no matter how they try to knock you down. There's a prayer I love, the twenty-third psalm:

The lord is my shepherd, I shall not want. He maketh me to lie down in green pastures; He leadeth me beside the still waters. Yay though I walk through the valley of the shadow of death, I shall fear no evil, for Thou art with me. Thy rod and thy staff, they comforteth me. Thou hast prepared a table before me in the presence of mine enemies; thou hast annointed my head with oil and my cup surely runneth over. Surely, Your goodness and mercy shall follow me all the days of my life, and I will dwell in the House of the Lord forever and ever.

Yes, I keep that on my mind all the time, because if you truly understand what that is saying, nothing can stop you. No one can stop me because I know my Father, and I am going to keep trusting in Jesus.

I have been hurt. I think we've all been hurt. But I am truly thankful for where I am today. I miss my daddy so much! I wish I had him here right now, but I know that God needed him as one of His angels. I miss my momma, Grandma Mason, Grandaddy Mason, Peter, and all my family and friends that have left this Earth behind to go dwell with Him in eternal peace. It's hard to express these feelings at times, but I know if I express the feelings I have inside of me, I will be free.

In the period of five years, I have lost three angles in my life. First, my granddaddy passed in August of 2004; my daddy passed in August of 2005; and finally Grandma Mason in May of 2009.

These losses were very hard on me, especially when Grandma Mason passed. I had been living with her for three years, and had taken as good a care of her as possible. She was at home recuperating after a minor surgery, and all seemed to be going well. She suddenly got very sick late one evening and passed the following morning.

From Grandma, I learned what it is like when someone has a total commitment to Jesus. Grandma never had an unkind word for anyone; even strangers who came upon trouble or ended up in the hospital would get a call or a visit from her. She was truly loved by everyone in her community

Granddaddy had degenerative arthritis, and had been sick for twenty years or more. He would not take any medications for his condition, insisting that "Doctor Jesus" would cure him if that was in the Divine Plan.

Daddy suffered from congestive heart failure; I took care of him throughout his illness and was present in the hospital room when he passed. I was always trying to model my life after daddy, who had overcome his demons and had gone on to lead a good and productive life as a husband and father.

Where in the past this might have led to bouts of depression, drugs, and alcohol, I was able to accept their passing from my life because I have come to have a personal relationship with Jesus. I have a new acceptance of death as a part of life, and a new assurance that there are blessings on the other side.

I am so honored to be alive today and to know how to deal with all of my feelings. But I shall not tolerate my negative feelings. As I always say in my meetings when we talk about anger, "I am able to deal with my anger, but I shall not tolerate my anger. I am able to deal with my negative feelings, but I won't tolerate those feelings; I am able to deal with my happiness, and I will tolerate my happiness!" And my love, and my joy, and my peace!

I'm not ashamed anymore, but I still hurt. I'm only human. It's like Jesus said: "We may weep tonight, but joy comes in the morning." Sometimes I'm glad to feel empty because I don't like to be out in the world of sin, because I know what it costs me—a lot of pain.

I listen to my gospel music and my bible every day, whether I feel up or down. I call upon the people I know who love me, and I listen to the voices of the angels inside them, and their wings start spreading out over me. And they say, "I love you. I'm here for you. And, I understand you, my child." I don't have to say any names; they know who they are.

I close saying that I love you all. I pray that all who read this book not only enjoy what they read, but gain a glimpse of what they may journey to be. Remember that no one journey is ever complete until we reach that other side. Strive to make this journey your best, so that you may glorify our Lord in all you do.

I love you all. And you know this Love! "I Don't Blame You"

Effect Change
By Robert Cook

You can change one individual through love...
Effect, Effect Change!

Look at the change in you that results in growth
and development...
The change for which I aspire...
You took the negative change and turned into
something that can set free...
Effect, Effect, Effect Change!

Meaningful change results in more and more
growth...
And for change to be meaningful, you must
experience the positive in you...
Effect, Effect, Effect Change!

Feeling the power of the generated is greater and
greater than any words can describe...
Power of Love...Power of Beauty...Power of God...
Is the power in you...
Effect, Effect, Effect Change!

The world is changing and changing daily...
And there is no way—NO WAY—we can stop the process...
Nor reverse the process...
We have to anticipate change, and plan for change, and understand how to implement change...
Effect, Effect, Effect Change...
In YOU!

Because Change is the essence of life!

Everybody Needs Somebody
By Robert Cook

No! No! No! No!
No words can ease the sorrow that you are deeply
going through!

No!

So many treasured loving memories, as long as
time endures...
Just Remember

Remember how much you mean to me. You are
surrounded by Angels...
Angels of Love all around you.

Angel of Love...Angel of Happiness...Angel of
Peace.
To bring you comfort when you are lost...

Just remember when we first fell in love. I can't
help but smiling each time I remember...

But most of all I remember the butterflies in my heart!

We started the journey so long ago, with nothing but dreams...

Now as we travel the journey of life...
Hand in Hand...
The love between us grows.

How wonderful it is that I have you to continue this journey,
With nothing but love, love, love to guide us on the way!
Love: the sweetest gift of all!

I am Happy, Happy, Happy that my somebody is you!

My Thoughts
By Robert Cook

I always wonder where my life is going, and where it's going to end. I have always thought that I am not worthy. I don't want to be here, but I keep my mind on Jesus. I know he told me that, if I took my life, I would burn in hell eternally. He wants to take it when it's time.

I fight the battles with thoughts like these, but I know what Jesus said. Jesus knows your thoughts before you even try to think them, but remember, I am just human. I am just a dirty, filthy rag. I wish I could just go into a little box and play with that little child that I once was, hiding to put myself in a place of love.

What is love? Love is happiness, joy.... See, Robert had to become Mr. Happy, because encouraging others also encourages me. Remember that Mr. Happy is just a character. In this journey I have been through, bad thoughts tried to take over my mind, but they can't, because I constantly pray.

I call people just to hear their voices, so I won't feel so empty. Sometimes I am alone, but I know that I am not supposed to be afraid. But I am afraid of death. I have had lots of death dreams clouding my thoughts. When I wake up, my heart is just pounding and racing and I am constantly seeing my dad. I try to block it out, but God wants me to face it.

I don't want to complain or to hurt anyone. I just want to be loved as I love others. God helps me each and every day to keep my mind on him. He has a divine plan for me, but once again, I am only human.

I am the dirty, filthy rag.

Appendix
Other Voices

By Christopher Barber
18 October 2002

Spoken into confusion
By thoughts controlling your mind
You don't know what to say
Or what to believe
Mislead and misguided
From what happened today
So you run away and hide
Friends become enemies
I don't blame you
It's not your fault

Faith became an illusion
'Cause no one can feel your pain
You want to be understood
It's for your own good
Dismayed and led away
It's how life's shaped & sized
I heard you on the inside
Calling for attention
I don't blame you
It's not your fault

Feelings of distance
Invade your world around you
It's been hard to figure out
It's heard in the way you sound
Unanswered and unheard
Don't that sound absurd?
At least you know who loves you
Does it take some pain away?
I don't blame you
It's not your fault

'Cause I'm not against you
So hold my hand and don't be scared
I'll never forsake you
Believe in me, don't live in fear
I don't blame you; it's not your fault
I'm here to pick you up
Lift you up off the ground
I'll never leave your side
I'll love you when you're down

BE WHO YOU ARE: *BY JOE CURRAN, MY GODSON, and MY FRIEND DON'S NEPHEW*

I adopted Don's nieces and nephews as my own. You never know what kind of an impact you will have on younger people, though. So I was deeply moved when Greg's youngest boy Joe wrote about me as a project for his tenth grade English class. His essay was called "The Difference."

"The first time I would see this man he walked into the room with such confidence. It was the first time my family would meet this man. I was going through a lot over that past year with friends and he made it change just by being there.

Robert is the man of honor and knows that with his wisdom he will be respected. He is the kind of man that has a myriad of ways even during the darkest hour to show the light which he preaches to all. Most of all his confidence shown through his colored skin in a town that is a population of whites. His style is none other and he is one in a million.

He showed me how to be me and to make people accept me for who I am like he made people accept him."

BY MY BROTHER GEORGE, MY FRIEND FROM MINNEAPOLIS

"When I think of Robert, I think of the brother I never had. I have never met anyone who could not only listen, but actually hear what I was saying. With his ability of listening I believe that he has helped me in a lot of situations. I feel like he has given me valuable insight that has guided me in the right direction in life. I am very fortunate to have met such a wonderful individual. To you Robert I say, "Thank You" for all you have done for me in my life."

BY MY ANGEL KELLY, CASE MANAGER AT GREAT LAKES TREATMENT CENTER

"I am very fortunate to have crossed the path of Mr. Robert Cooks. He is always calling people 'Angel' however, I believe he is an angel sent to us in disguise. His courage, wisdom, values, and beliefs have intrigued me and are extremely refreshing. I have an enormous amount of respect for Robert and I know he has and will continue to impact other's lives in an incredible way. I will always remember Robert and think of him as my 'Angel.'"

BY MARK, A GOOD FRIEND FROM DETROIT, MICHIGAN.

I met Mark on the Internet. It didn't take me long to realize that he was a quiet, spiritual person. When I visited with him, I saw that his home is full of motivational videos! I'd like to share a letter Mark wrote to me:

"Where do I begin? I suppose that it is imperative that I express to you that in the short time since our meeting, it has seemed as though we are two old souls who have known each other before. Our acquaintance has been more of a period of "catching up" since the familiarity we share, rather uncannily, is so apparent.

To know someone who has been so blessed is (*in itself*) a blessing. Your positive outlook on life is contagious and your zeal is infectious. You have surrounded yourself with people who have so positively affected your life, and in return, that positive environment perpetuates itself daily in everything you do. Though I cannot imagine the pain in your past, I am amazed by the fact that you have transcended it and that you possess such a positive outlook and caring heart.

The directness with which you interact is amazing. There are no inhibitions to keep you from allowing yourself to feel and express those feelings. You say that you read people, this is a gift, though I'm sure it presents its occasional dichotomies. Yet, you remain undaunted by the complexity and simply draw out the nature of an individual in short order and with ruthless unequivocality. Though some people may be taken aback by that, I find it to be a refreshing change from the usual phoniness with which most of us approach people. Though you are unapologetic for your observations, you are still sensitive to people's feelings.

While getting acquainted, you have shown me that you do not allow others the luxury of expressing themselves without first substantiating their feelings. There are no easy or pat answers, as you force others to verbalize their individual truths. I believe that you are destined to accomplish great things in this life. You impact people with the force of a roaring train, unwavering and powerful. I am glad that we have had this opportunity to get better acquainted. Speaking strictly for myself, I confess a certain envy of your direct nature and the confidence you exude. Though, I do not know the extent to which our lives will interact from this point forward, I am sure that my life will be changed immeasurably based upon our friendship. To be sure, getting to know you may not be an easy task, but I am assured that it will be a fulfilling one.

I am honored by your willingness to go out of your way to "want" to get to know me. My self-image has been damaged by the trials of my life and you have shown me that I have value not just as a friend, but as a brother. That sense of being needed and cared for has recently been rejuvenated and was long overdue in my life. To be appreciated for who I am (*not just what I may or may not be able to offer*) is a powerful healing to my self-worth and though we may not agree on all things, the acceptance of my positions shows that you care more for me than you care for winning a debate. I respect that more than you will ever know.

We've discussed many ideas and concepts in our brief introduction and I trust that we will be afforded many more opportunities to do so in the future. I am pleased to have you in my life and I wish you only the best in your future and hope that you will continue to view me in the same undaunted spirit. "The Lord watch between me and thee, when we are absent one from another." (Gen 31:49)"

From "Ma" Dianne Perkins

Who was this gorgeous, tall black man who walked so confidently into our shop and said he was checking out the competition? He appeared very cheerful and flamboyant. My brother had just about the same personality, which was really what attracted me to him like a magnet. As fast as he walked in, he was gone. So I followed him around the corner to his shop. I walked in and introduced myself; we talked and exchanged phone numbers. This was the start of one of the best friendships of my life.

Robert had quite a large drinking problem, I found out as we got to know one another. But he made up for it by being cheerful, multi-talented, considerate and the list can go on. Robert would go out at night and party. During the day, he would have a hard time getting up for work and making his appointments. He had a list of problems from earlier in his life, which I knew about.

Robert came on a little too strong for people in this rather quiet community. Not too many people had open minds. I knew I had to try and help my friend, but I didn't exactly know how. So I thought just by being there all the time for him was my way of helping him. He would call me at times when he got home from being out at night and sings his heart out. Robert was very kind hearted and that made him very vulnerable to many different kinds of people in town—none of them very good. He was beaten up—money taken from him. He would also feel sorry for people and give them too many things.

Push came to shove and Robert left town, but our friendship kept going. He moved to Escanaba for a while and then moved back to Saginaw. It was after he moved to Saginaw for a while—probably a span of four years—when I began to see a big change in him. He moved in with Grandma, who was a wonderful woman, and started going to church with her and her friends. With a lot of work and determination, he got control of his drinking and began doing many positive things in his life.

He loves to sing, dance and write. He visits the sick and elderly people in hospitals and cheers them up. He has a radio show. His talents just keep coming out. He doesn't drink any more and has more responsibilities. He has come to a peaceful feeling of who he is. To me, Robert will always be my best friend and inspiration. He was sent to me at a time when I needed him. He is truly the most wonderful person I have ever met. He is intelligent and very determined to keep making himself better and has overcome many obstacles in his life. Robert is truly, to everyone who really knows him, a blessing in life.

69540114R00063